MVFOL

BL: 6.7
AR Pts: 1.0

American Moments

ABDO
& Daughters

THE TRAIL OF TEARS

By Alan Pierce

VISIT US AT
WWW.ABDOPUB.COM

Published by ABDO Publishing Company, 4940 Viking Drive, Suite 622, Edina, Minnesota 55435. Copyright © 2005 by Abdo Consulting Group, Inc. International copyrights reserved in all countries. No part of this book may be reproduced in any form without written permission from the publisher. ABDO & Daughters™ is a trademark and logo of ABDO Publishing Company.

Printed in the United States.

Edited by: Melanie A. Howard
Interior Production and Design: Terry Dunham Incorporated
Cover Design: Mighty Media
Photos: Corbis, Library of Congress, Woolaroc Museum

Library of Congress Cataloging-in-Publication Data

Pierce, Alan, 1966-
 The Trail of Tears / Alan Pierce.
  p. cm. -- (American moments)
 Includes index.
 ISBN 1-59197-736-3
 1. Trail of Tears, 1838. 2. Cherokee Indians--Relocation. 3. Cherokee Indians--History.
4. Cherokee Indians--Government relations. I. Title. II. Series.

E99.C5P46 2005
736'.6--dc22

                                                        2004046288

CONTENTS

THE TRAIL WHERE THEY CRIED

In 1839, a traveler in Kentucky reported a grim sight. He encountered hundreds of suffering Native Americans moving west. Some walked without shoes on the cold ground. The sick and the weak rode in wagons. With almost every stop, the Native Americans buried more than a dozen people. The Native Americans in this wagon train were Cherokee who had been forced to leave their land in the southeastern United States. Several groups of Cherokee departed in the fall and traveled during the winter.

A Native American man who made this journey in the snow later recounted the suffering. He remembered the women, children, and men crying as they proceeded west. In their own language the Cherokee called the route nuh-NO-hee doo-na-DLO-hyi-luh. It means "the trail where they cried." This became known as the Trail of Tears. The phrase refers to the 800-mile (1,287-km) journey the Cherokee made from their homeland to present-day Oklahoma.

The Cherokee had recently been part of a thriving nation. Many had become farmers. The Cherokee also operated stores, blacksmith shops, and sawmills. In fact, in the 1830s, Cherokee settlements and white

The Trail of Tears *by Robert Lindneux illustrates the Cherokee removal.*

villages were similar. And yet, the Cherokee were forced to leave their homes for land in the west. The Cherokee embarked on their long march because the U.S. government was dedicated to moving Native Americans west of the Mississippi River. The country followed that policy even though it led to the Trail of Tears.

American Moments

FIVE TRIBES

The Cherokee dwelled in what is now the southeastern United States. Other prominent tribes were the Chickasaw, Choctaw, and Creek. These tribes had inhabited this region for centuries. The Spanish explorer Hernando de Soto had met all four tribes when he explored the area in 1540-1541.

Although the four tribes lived in the same region of North America, they had their own areas. The Cherokee lived primarily in present-day Georgia, northern Alabama, and parts of Tennessee and North Carolina. South of the Cherokee were the Creek, called Muskogee in their language. They lived mainly in what is now Georgia and Alabama. The Chickasaw were located in present-day northern Mississippi, although they expanded their territory north and west. Choctaw villages were found in southern and central Mississippi.

The region where these tribes lived was wooded and featured many river valleys. These characteristics influenced how the Native Americans lived. For example, the Cherokee built log homes and located their villages along rivers. The Chickasaw also lived near rivers, but their settlements were more spread out.

All four tribes farmed the rich soil of this region. They grew corn, beans, and squash. Among the Native Americans in this region,

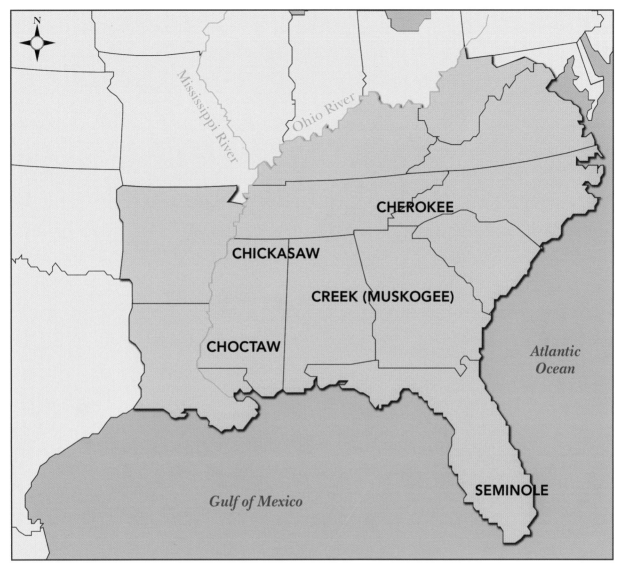

*This map shows the locations of the
Five Civilized Tribes before the Trail of Tears.*

the Choctaw were considered the finest farmers. They worked the productive soil along the Mississippi River.

In the eighteenth century, a fifth tribe formed. This tribe was called the Seminole. They were members of the Creek tribe who had moved from Georgia into what was then the Spanish territory of Florida. The Seminole also farmed, but they acquired most of their food by hunting and fishing.

COLONIZATION AND CONQUEST

Problems between Native Americans and whites began almost as soon as Europeans began to explore the Western Hemisphere in 1492. One serious misfortune was disease. European explorers and colonists exposed the Native Americans to smallpox and other diseases. Native Americans were not immune to these illnesses. In some areas, 90 percent of the Native American population died from disease.

Native Americans also had to deal with Europeans moving onto their land. In the sixteenth and seventeenth centuries, Spain, France, Holland, Sweden, and England established colonies in North America. In 1607, England founded its first successful colony in North America. It was established on the James River in the territory of Virginia. The settlement was named Jamestown after England's King James I.

Throughout the seventeenth and eighteenth centuries, more English settlers arrived in the North American colonies. By 1732, England established the last of its 13 colonies along the Atlantic coast. It was named Georgia after England's King George II.

The Native Americans became drawn into the struggles between England and France in North America. In addition to settling what is now Canada, France also claimed the vast Louisiana Territory in the North American interior. In 1754, England and France went to war over control of the Ohio River valley.

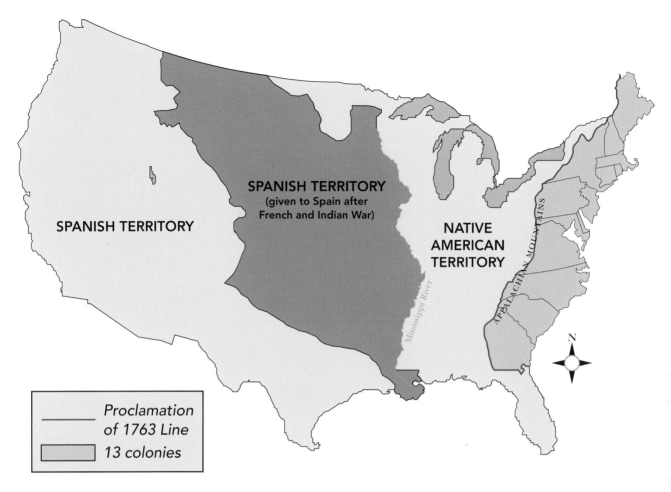

SPANISH TERRITORY

SPANISH TERRITORY
(given to Spain after
French and Indian War)

NATIVE
AMERICAN
TERRITORY

APPALACHIAN MOUNTAINS

Mississippi River

N

Proclamation
of 1763 Line

13 colonies

*This map shows the western boundaries of the 13 colonies fixed
at the Appalachian Mountains after the Proclamation of 1763.*

At first, the Cherokee were allied with the English against the
French. However, after settlers killed 12 Cherokee, a few Cherokee
leaders began attacking the English. The Cherokee gained some
victories against the English. But ultimately, the English vanquished
both the French and the Cherokee in what came to be known as the
French and Indian War.

After the war ended, England's King George III issued the
Proclamation of 1763. This proclamation barred English colonists
from settling west of the Appalachian Mountains. England made the
proclamation to prevent more costly wars with the Native Americans.

However, England also compelled the Cherokee to give up land east of these mountains. Despite the king's proclamation, settlers continued to push west onto Cherokee land. Violations of the king's order made the Cherokee resent the colonists.

The Cherokee were drawn into another war in 1775. By this time, the colonies had revolted against British rule. In the Revolutionary War between the 13 American colonies and Britain, the Cherokee supported the British. In 1776, the colonists invaded Cherokee land and destroyed the Native Americans' homes and food supply. This campaign forced most of the Cherokee out of the war.

In 1781, the colonies won the war when the British surrendered at Yorktown in Virginia. The independence of the United States was realized with the Treaty of Paris in 1783. This treaty also extended the western border of the United States to the Mississippi River.

The British surrender at Yorktown, Virginia.

The Cherokee, Chickasaw, Choctaw, and Creek now all lived within the borders claimed by the new United States.

The U.S. government debated how to deal with the Native Americans within its borders. One idea was assimilation. This meant changing Native American culture so that it was similar to white culture. More specifically, assimilation called for Native Americans to use white methods of farming and to take up white trades. The government hoped assimilation would cause Native Americans to live on less land.

In the 1790s, the U.S. government took steps to motivate Native Americans to adopt white agricultural practices. For example, in the Treaty of Holston, the United States promised to give farm equipment to the Cherokee. The government also began setting aside money every year to buy livestock and farm implements for the Native Americans.

At this time, the Cherokee also began to follow the white practice of owning slaves. Blacks from Africa had been used as slaves in the American colonies and the United States for about 200 years. Slavery had ended for the most part in the northern United States by the nineteenth century. However, slavery remained strong in the South. Cotton was grown in the South, and slaves were used to plant and harvest cotton.

Many whites in the United States, however, did not want to see the Native Americans assimilated. Whites who held these views tended to live on the frontier where wars with Native Americans had taken place. These settlers saw Native Americans as a threat that should be removed or killed. Also, some whites held racist beliefs about the Native Americans. In their view, Native Americans were incapable of adapting to white culture.

American Moments

WAR OF 1812

After the Revolutionary War, the western borders of the states needed to be determined. Some states claimed land that extended to the Mississippi River. In a few cases, two states claimed the same area. Georgia did not assert ownership of land claimed by another state. But Georgia did assume possession of territory that now makes up much of Alabama and Mississippi.

In 1802, the federal government and Georgia worked out an agreement. The arrangement called for Georgia to give up its claims to the western territory. In return, the federal government paid Georgia $1.25 million. But the federal government also made another promise. It pledged to obtain land held by Native Americans within Georgia's borders.

Acquiring Native American land was not simple. In the 1790s, the federal government began to treat Native American tribes as sovereign nations. This policy meant that the United States did not always use force to get land from Native Americans. Instead, the United States attempted to buy land and make treaties with tribes.

This U.S. policy toward the tribes did not eliminate proposals to move Native Americans further west. In fact, the idea for moving Native Americans gained some momentum in 1803. In that year, the United States purchased the Louisiana Territory from France. The addition of this territory gave the United States 828,000 square

Thomas Jefferson

miles (2.1 million sq km) of land west of the Mississippi River. President Thomas Jefferson wanted Native Americans in the eastern United States to move to this territory.

Native Americans later became involved in the conflict between the United States and Great Britain. One source of the hostility was British military support for Native American leader Tecumseh. He was a Shawnee chief who worked to form a Native American confederacy. Tecumseh wanted to use this confederacy to fight American settlers in the Ohio River valley.

The Louisiana Territory doubled the size of the United States.

LOUISIANA TERRITORY

Mississippi River

Ohio River

N

Disagreements about shipping also contributed to the hostility between Britain and the United States. The British interfered with U.S. ships and forced U.S. sailors to join the British navy. Ultimately, the dispute over shipping and British support of Native Americans led to the War of 1812. On June 18, 1812, the U.S. Congress declared war against Britain.

Many Native Americans saw the war as a chance to strike out against the United States. Tecumseh had influenced Native Americans in the South. Some members of the Creek tribe believed in his struggle against the United States. These Creek were known as Red Sticks. They were called this because when war broke out, the Creek set up a red pole. But not all the Creek joined the Red Sticks. Those who did not join the Red Sticks were known as White Sticks.

On July 27, 1813, the U.S. militia surprised the Red Sticks in present-day Alabama. The Red Sticks drove back the U.S. troops. Not many people were killed in the fight called the Battle of Burnt Corn Creek. But the fighting alarmed the White Sticks and white settlers, who feared the Red Sticks might attack them. The White Sticks, the settlers, and their slaves went to Fort Mims for protection. This fort was about 20 miles (32 km) north of Mobile.

Slaves reported seeing Native Americans outside the fort, but these warnings were ignored. On August 30, the Red Sticks attacked Fort Mims. They slew about 500 White Sticks and American settlers and took the slaves prisoner.

The massacre provoked a U.S. military response. U.S. forces invaded from Georgia, Tennessee, and what is now Mississippi. General Andrew Jackson of Tennessee led the largest force of 5,000 militiamen. His army also included White Sticks and about 600 Cherokee.

Among these Cherokee were leaders such as Major Ridge and John Ross. Ridge was a Cherokee warrior who had become a prosperous farmer. Ross was 23 years old, but already he had been involved with the Cherokee council.

Shawnee chief Tecumseh

Meanwhile, the Red Sticks assembled in the village of Tohopeka. This village was built on a bend in the Tallapoosa River in what is now Alabama. The river provided a natural defense. To further secure the village, the Red Sticks built a 1,200-foot-long (366-m) barricade made of logs. This barricade was constructed to guard against an attack from land.

On March 27, 1814, Jackson's force attacked the village. Militia and U.S. troops assaulted the barricade. Cherokee and Creek warriors in Jackson's army swam across the river to attack the village. In seven hours of fighting, Jackson's forces killed about 800 Red Stick warriors. Jackson was almost killed in the fighting. But Cherokee chief Junaluska rescued the general from a Creek warrior armed with a tomahawk.

Jackson's victory over the Red Sticks became known as the Battle of Horseshoe Bend, also called the Battle of Tohopeka. This battle made Jackson a war hero. But it was a devastating loss for the Red Sticks. The battle shattered their ability to wage war against the United States.

In August, Jackson met with representatives of the Creek tribe at Fort Jackson in present-day Alabama. Most of the Creek who met with Jackson were allies of the United States. Those still hostile to the United States had escaped to Spain's territory in Florida.

At the meeting, Jackson presented a treaty that obligated the Creek to give 23 million acres (9 million ha) to the United States. This region included land in southern Georgia. It also included about three-fifths of the area that would make up what is now Alabama. Jackson told the Creeks that if they did not sign the treaty they would have to move to Florida. On August 9, the Creeks signed the Treaty of Fort Jackson.

ANDREW JACKSON – "OLD HICKORY"

During the War of 1812, Andrew Jackson was given the nickname "Old Hickory" because he was tough like hickory wood. Democrats later used his nickname in the 1824 election to support Jackson's presidential campaign. Images of hickory trees were put on buttons, hats, canes, and even brooms to represent Jackson's campaign, and were given to his supporters. Jackson lost the 1824 presidential election to John Quincy Adams. The race had been so close that the U.S. House of Representatives decided the winner.

ASSIMILATION

The War of 1812 convinced many Native Americans that fighting against the United States was hopeless. Instead, assimilation seemed a more promising way to save their land. In the South, the Cherokee in particular became successful at conforming to white culture.

One way that Native Americans adopted white culture was by establishing English-speaking schools. Religious groups helped establish many of these schools. For example, the American Board of Commissioners for Foreign Missions helped found the Brainerd school. It was established in 1817 in southeast Tennessee and became the most prominent Cherokee school.

In 1819, Congress began what was called the Civilization Fund. The government disbursed money from this fund to religious organizations. These organizations used the money to set up more schools for Native Americans. The Cherokee, Chickasaw, Choctaw, and Creek all gained schools because of the Civilization Fund. The schools helped these four tribes along with the Seminole become known as the Five Civilized Tribes.

These English-speaking schools did not cause the Cherokee to neglect their own language. A Cherokee man named Sequoyah developed a syllabary of 86 symbols that stood for syllables in the Cherokee language. Sequoyah showed his writing system to the

Sequoyah holding the Cherokee syllabary

Cherokee Alphabet

D *a*	R *e*	T *i*	Ꮄ *o*	O *u*	i *v*
S *ga* O *ka*	Ᏺ *ge*	Ᏻ *gi*	A *go*	J *gu*	E *gv*
Ᏸ *ha*	Ᏺ *he*	Ᏸ *hi*	Ᏺ *ho*	Ᏺ *hu*	Ᏸ *hv*
W *la*	Ꮄ *le*	Ꮅ *li*	G *lo*	M *lu*	Ꮖ *lv*
Ᏽ *ma*	Ꮍ *me*	H *mi*	Ꮞ *mo*	Y *mu*	
O *na* Ꮤ *hna* G *nah*	Ꮑ *ne*	Ꭸ *ni*	Z *no*	Ꮩ *nu*	O *nv*
T *qua*	ꙍ *que*	Ꮖ *qui*	V *quo*	Ꮸ *quu*	Ꮛ *quv*
U *sa* ꝏ *s*	4 *se*	Ᏸ *si*	Ꮸ *so*	Ᏽ *su*	R *sv*
Ᏸ *da* W *ta*	Ꮝ *de* Ꮧ *te*	Ꮨ *di* Ꮅ *ti*	Λ *do*	S *du*	Ᏸ *dv*
Ꮪ *dla* Ꮣ *tla*	Ꮮ *tle*	C *tli*	Ꮖ *tlo*	Ꮹ *tlu*	P *tlv*
Ꮎ *tsa*	Ꮴ *tse*	Ꮪ *tsi*	K *tso*	J *tsu*	C *tsv*
G *wa*	Ꮿ *we*	Ꮻ *wi*	Ꮼ *wo*	Ꮿ *wu*	6 *wv*
Ꮿ *ya*	Ᏸ *ye*	Ꮹ *yi*	Ꮿ *yo*	G *yu*	B *yv*

Sounds represented by vowels.

a as *a* in *father* or short as *a* in *rival*   o as *aw* in *law* or short as *o* in *not*
e as *a* in *hate* or short as *e* in *met*   u as *oo* in *fool* or short as *u* in *pull*
i as *i* in *pique* or short as *i* in *pit*   v as *u* in *but*, nasalized.

Consonant Sounds.

g nearly as in English, but approaching to k. _ d nearly as in English, but approaching to t. _ h, k, l, m, n, q, s, t, w, y, as in English.
Syllables beginning with g, except Ꮝ have sometimes the power of k, a, s, w, are sometimes sounded to, tu, tv, and syllables written with tl,
except Ꮣ, sometimes vary to dl.

TRAIL OF TEARS IN CHEROKEE

Ꮕ Z Ꭿ   Ꮪ Ꮎ Ꮣ Ᏺ Ꮈ

nv – no – hi   du – na – dlo – yi – lv

Sounds like: *nuh – NO – hee   doo – na – DLO – hyi – luh*

Cherokee chiefs in 1821. They approved the syllabary, and thousands of Cherokee learned to read and write in their own language.

Education and a written language were not the only ways that the Cherokee adopted white culture. The Cherokee had been farmers for centuries, but now they farmed like other whites in the South. They raised thousands of cattle, sheep, and swine. In addition, they grew corn, wheat, and cotton.

Moreover, some Cherokee continued to own slaves. According to an 1824 census, there were 1,277 slaves in the Cherokee Nation. However, ownership of slaves was not widespread among the Cherokee. A later census indicated that 96 families out of 1,357 owned slaves.

The third way that the Cherokee adopted white culture was government. In 1817, the Cherokee established a form of government that was similar to the U.S. federal government. Both systems of government had legislative, executive, and judicial branches.

Meanwhile, conflict between Native Americans and the United States continued. In 1817, Andrew Jackson fought the First Seminole War. He led a U.S. invasion to capture runaway slaves in Spain's territory of Florida. Many of these slaves lived with the Seminole. Jackson's invasion eventually led to Florida becoming part of the United States.

The Cherokee success with assimilation, however, did not stop plans to move Native Americans west. In the 1820s, the U.S. government referred to the region west of Missouri and the Arkansas Territory as "Indian Country." Some hoped to avoid more conflict over land by moving the Native Americans to this western area.

REMOVAL ACT

The dispute between Georgia and the Cherokee Nation reached a turning point in 1827. In that year, the Cherokee legislature adopted a constitution based on the laws of the U.S. Constitution. However, the Cherokee Constitution also made an important claim. It said the Cherokee Nation was "sovereign and independent."

Many Georgians were angry about the Cherokee claim of sovereignty. Georgia had waited since 1802 for the federal government to expel the Cherokee. It did not matter to these Georgians that the Cherokee had adopted white ways. They hoped to gain the Cherokee land and saw the Cherokee Constitution as a threat to this goal.

The conflicts between the Cherokee Nation and its white neighbors were recorded in the newspaper the *Cherokee Phoenix*. A Cherokee man named Elias Boudinot began publishing the newspaper in February 1828. The newspaper printed articles in both Cherokee and English. Boudinot used the newspaper to reproach white people for their desire for Cherokee land.

In 1828, Georgia gained an important ally in its effort to drive out the Cherokee. Andrew Jackson was elected president of the United States. He supported removal of Native Americans. After Jackson became president, Georgia claimed jurisdiction over 9 million acres

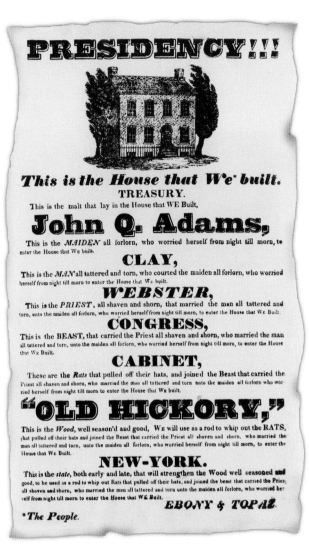

PRESIDENCY!!!

This is the House that We· built.

TREASURY.

This is the malt that lay in the House that WE Built,

John Q. Adams,

This is the *MAIDEN* all forlorn, who worried herself from night till morn, to enter the House that We built.

CLAY,

This is the *MAN* all tattered and torn, who courted the maiden all forlorn, who worried herself from night till morn to enter the House that We built.

WEBSTER,

This is the *PRIEST*, all shaven and shorn, that married the man all tattered and torn, unto the maiden all forlorn, who worried herself from night till morn, to enter the House that We Built.

CONGRESS,

This is the BEAST, that carried the Priest all shaven and shorn, who married the man all tattered and torn, unto the maiden all forlorn, who worried herself from night till morn, to enter the House that We Built.

CABINET,

These are the *Rats* that pulled off their hats, and joined the Beast that carried the Priest all shaven and shorn, who married the man all tattered and torn unto the maiden all forlorn who worried herself from night till morn to enter the House that We built.

"OLD HICKORY,"

This is the *Wood*, well season'd and good, We will use as a rod to whip out the RATS, that pulled off their hats and joined the Beast that carried the Priest all shaven and shorn, who married the man all tattered and torn, unto the maiden all forlorn, who worried herself from night till morn, to enter the House that We Built.

NEW-YORK.

This is the *state*, both early and late, that will strengthen the Wood well seasoned and good, to be used as a rod to whip out Rats that pulled off their hats, and joined the beast that carried the Priest all shaven and shorn, who married the man all tattered and torn unto the maiden all forlorn, who worried herself from night till morn to enter the House that We Built.

EBONY & TOPAZ.

*The People.

A poster from Andrew Jackson's presidential campaign

(3.6 million ha) of land inhabited by the Cherokee. The Georgia legislature passed laws that extended the power of Georgia's courts over the Cherokee Nation. Georgia's new laws also did not recognize the authority of the Cherokee's tribal government. Jackson supported Georgia's actions.

The desire for land increased the conflict between Georgia and the Cherokee Nation. Whites coveted the land in the southern United States because of the high demand for cotton. This crop had become profitable because of the Industrial Revolution in Great Britain and the United States. In both countries, factories had been built that used tremendous amounts of cotton to make cloth. At this time, the southern United States provided a large amount of the world's cotton.

The Cherokee Nation also occupied an important location. This land cut Georgia off from the Tennessee River. Access to the Tennessee River was considered critical because it flowed into the Ohio and Mississippi rivers. If Georgia had access to the Tennessee

River, then the state would have access to more markets. Some people imagined using a railroad to link Georgia's agricultural area with the Tennessee River.

In July 1829, an event occurred that further increased demand for Cherokee land. Gold was discovered near Dahlonega in the Cherokee Nation. White miners swarmed over the Cherokee land, although federal troops were supposed to keep them out. Meanwhile, the Georgia legislature made it illegal for Native Americans to mine for gold.

President Jackson pushed the federal government to take stronger action to remove the Native Americans. In December 1829, he delivered his State of the Union address. During this speech, he supported the idea of removing the Native Americans west of the Mississippi River. Jackson said removal should be voluntary. But Native Americans who remained in the eastern United States should expect to follow state laws.

Congress debated a bill to move Native Americans in 1830. The bill called for setting up the Indian Territory west of the Mississippi River. This territory was the region formerly known as Indian Country. Native American land in the east would be traded for land in Indian Territory.

The bill provoked a lot of debate in the country. Religious organizations and charities collected petitions against the removal bill. Also, many women expressed their opposition to the removal bill by sending petitions to Congress. Jackson's supporters formed their own group that favored removal.

Like the country, Congress was divided over the removal bill. Members of Congress in the northern and eastern states tended to oppose the bill. Those in the southern and western states were

DID YOU KNOW?

Did you know that Davy Crockett voted against the Removal Act of 1830? Crockett was a famous frontiersman and author who served in the U.S. House of Representatives during Andrew Jackson's term. In 1830, Andrew Jackson sent a bill to Congress that would authorize the removal of Native Americans, such as the Cherokee, from their native lands. Crockett opposed this bill, even though many of his supporters told him that it would ruin his political career. Crockett, however, still contested the bill, stating that it was a "wicked, unjust measure" and that he would "go against it, let the cost . . . be what it might." Jackson's political party successfully kept Crockett from being reelected in 1835. Crockett then left Washington DC and traveled to Texas, where he died in the Battle of the Alamo in March 1836.

Davy Crockett

more likely to favor it. On April 23, the Senate voted 28-19 to approve the bill. In May, the House of Representatives approved the bill 102-97. Jackson signed the legislation, which became known as the Indian Removal Act or Removal Act.

THE REMOVAL

The Indian Removal Act first affected the Choctaw, Chickasaw, Creek, and Seminole. U.S. officials negotiated with the Choctaw. In order to get a treaty, officials bribed some Choctaw leaders with promises of land in the state of Mississippi. On September 27, 1830, the United States and Choctaw signed the Treaty of Dancing Rabbit Creek. This treaty ceded 11 million acres (4.5 million ha) of Choctaw land in Mississippi to the United States. In exchange, the Choctaw received about 15 million acres (6.1 million ha) of land in what is now southern Oklahoma.

Soon after the treaty, many Choctaw began to emigrate to their new territory. Those who moved during the winter suffered from cold and hunger. Those who moved west in the summer also endured hardship. Cholera was a major health problem at the time. It is estimated that 4,000 Choctaw died from cholera during the move west. In total, about 9,000 Choctaw traveled to the Indian Territory in the 1830s.

Next, the federal government negotiated with the Chickasaw to buy land in Mississippi and Alabama. A treaty was worked out in 1832, but the Chickasaw could not move yet. The Chickasaw were expected to settle on land purchased from the Choctaw in Indian Territory. Meanwhile, whites began intruding on Chickasaw land. In 1837, an agreement with the Choctaw was reached and the Chickasaw began their move west.

Members of the Cherokee Nation

The Chickasaw journey was less hazardous. By this time the U.S. government was better prepared to move the Native Americans. The Chickasaw received more clothes and blankets for the trek. There were also new roads to assist with travel. In the 1830s, about 6,000 Chickasaw moved to their new land in the Indian Territory. But the Chickasaw still suffered. Once they arrived, a number of Chickasaw died of cholera.

The Indian Removal Act also affected the Seminole because Florida had become part of the United States. In 1832, the United States negotiated a removal treaty with this tribe. The Seminole were starving because of a drought and agreed to move if the land in the west was found to be acceptable. Some Seminole traveled to Indian

Territory to examine the land. They signed an agreement that obligated the tribe to move within three years.

Seminole leaders in Florida argued against the agreement. Still, some Seminole moved west. But most stayed in Florida and began fighting against the United States in 1835. A Seminole leader named Osceola helped lead attacks against U.S. forces. The Seminole withdrew to the forests and swamps of the Everglades where they continued to fight. In 1837, General T.S. Jesup captured Osceola during a truce. Osceola died of malaria in captivity. But the Seminole kept up their resistance.

In 1832, the Creek also negotiated a treaty to cede their land to the United States. Like the Choctaw and the Chickasaw, they would receive land in Indian Territory. However, thousands of whites entered Creek land and began to destroy the tribe's property before the Creek had left. The federal government attempted to use troops to stop the trespassers. This action led to a conflict with the state of Alabama. Eventually, the state of Alabama agreed to protect Creek land.

Violence between the Creek and whites erupted in 1836. The U.S. military waged a swift campaign against the Creek. This act led to 3,000 Creek being shipped west on boats. Within the next year, about 18,000 Creek were sent west to settle in present-day central Oklahoma. Many of them moved west during the winter and suffered through harsh weather. No one is certain how many Creek died during their removal. Some estimates place the number of deaths between 3,500 and 10,000.

Osceola was a Seminole leader in the Second Seminole War. But he was not a chief. When some Seminole chiefs signed a treaty for removal, Osceola stabbed his knife through the treaty and said, "This is the only treaty I will make with the whites!"

American Moments

SOVEREIGNTY ON TRIAL

While other tribes were moving west, the Cherokee fought in the courts for their sovereignty. The Cherokee Nation and the state of Georgia were still clashing over the matter of jurisdiction. One conflict involved the murder case of a Native American named George Tassel. He was found guilty in Georgia state court of murder. Tassel, however, argued that Georgia did not have jurisdiction over a crime that occurred on Cherokee land.

The U.S. Supreme Court considered Tassel's claim in the case of *Georgia v. Tassel*. In 1830, the Supreme Court agreed with Tassel by ruling that his case should be retried in federal court. The state of Georgia rejected the Supreme Court's decision, and executed Tassel.

Georgia's actions prompted the Cherokee to initiate a lawsuit in federal court against the state of Georgia. The suit challenged Georgia's practice of applying state laws to the Cherokee. In 1831, the case called *Cherokee Nation v. State of Georgia* went to the U.S. Supreme Court.

In the suit, the Cherokee claimed their land was a foreign nation. Supreme Court justice John Marshall disagreed. Furthermore, he believed that Native American tribes could not bring cases to the Supreme Court. Therefore, Marshall declined to hear the case.

30

THE CASE

OF

THE CHEROKEE NATION

against

THF STATE OF GEORGIA:

ARGUED AND DETERMINED AT

THE SUPREME COURT OF THE UNITED STATES,

JANUARY TERM 1831.

WITH

AN APPENDIX,

Containing the Opinion of Chancellor Kent on the Case; the Treaties between
the United States and the Cherokee Indians; the Act of Congress of
1802, entitled 'An Act to regulate intercourse with the Indian
tribes, &c.'; and the Laws of Georgia relative to the
country occupied by the Cherokee Indians,
within the boundary of that State.

BY RICHARD PETERS,
COUNSELLOR AT LAW.

𝔓𝔥𝔦𝔩𝔞𝔡𝔢𝔩𝔭𝔥𝔦𝔞:

JOHN GRIGG, 9 NORTH FOURTH STREET.
1831.

*Title page of the U.S. Supreme Court record
of Cherokee Nation v. State of Georgia*

Georgia then passed more laws that affected the Cherokee Nation. One law compelled white men living on Native American land to have a license from the state. A missionary named Samuel Austin Worcester was living with the Cherokee. He was found in violation of this law and was arrested. The Superior Court in Georgia's Gwinnett County convicted Worcester and sentenced him to four years in prison.

The U.S. Supreme Court stepped in to consider the case of *Worcester v. Georgia*. On March 3, 1832, Justice Marshall issued the Court's decision. The Court ruled in favor of Worcester. Marshall wrote that Worcester's conviction was wrong because Georgia's laws did not apply to the territory of the Cherokee Nation. Instead, the Court ruled that only the federal government had authority over Native American nations.

Worcester v. Georgia was a legal triumph for the Cherokee. The U.S. Supreme Court had declared that the Cherokee Nation was free from Georgia's power. In reality, the case failed to help the Cherokee. Georgia ignored the Supreme Court's ruling and proceeded with a lottery to sell Cherokee land to settlers.

President Jackson also did not respect the Supreme Court's ruling. He was reported as saying, "Justice Marshall has made his decision, now let him enforce it." As president, Jackson was responsible for enforcing the ruling. But he had no intention of doing so, and he did not stop Georgia's actions to take over Cherokee land.

Opposite page: *Supreme Court justice John Marshall*

NEW ECHOTA

By this time, some Cherokee believed they would not be able to keep their land. Some leaders concluded that removal was the best course. These leaders were Boudinot, Chief Major Ridge, his son John Ridge, and nephew Stand Watie. This group, however, did not represent the wishes of most Cherokee. Also, Principal Chief John Ross opposed removal.

The division within the Cherokee Nation was evident by June 1834. In that month, a delegation of Cherokee traveled to Washington DC. The group was made up of Cherokee from the east and those who had already settled in the west. While in Washington DC, the group signed a removal treaty even though the delegation had no authority to do so. The Cherokee Nation's council rejected the treaty, and the U.S. Senate never ratified it.

In February 1835, John Ridge and other Cherokee negotiated a treaty with the U.S. government. The treaty would pay the Cherokee $4.5 million for their land east of the Mississippi River. Approval of the treaty depended on the Cherokee council accepting it. In October 1835, the council rejected the treaty.

After two failed attempts to secure a treaty, Georgia and the federal government had lost patience. The Georgia militia arrested Ross and held him in jail for a few days. He was not charged with any crime. The Cherokee were then told to appear in New Echota in December

Chief John Ross

to consider a treaty. Absent Cherokee would be counted as being in favor of removal. Only about 300 to 500 Cherokee men, women, and children traveled to New Echota for the treaty meeting.

The U.S. government and Cherokee who were present negotiated the Treaty of New Echota. The treaty stated that the Cherokee would receive $5 million for 7.9 million acres (3.2 million ha) of land east of the Mississippi River. They would also receive 7.8 million acres (3.2 million ha) in Indian Territory. In addition, they were given two years to move west. John Ross petitioned the Senate to reject the treaty. The U.S. Senate, however, ratified the treaty by one vote.

TRAIL OF TEARS

In 1837, hundreds of Cherokee left for the tribe's section of Indian Territory in what is now northeastern Oklahoma. Many of these Cherokee traveled on flatboats along the Tennessee, Ohio, Mississippi, and Arkansas rivers. No Cherokee died on these early migrations by water. But the flatboats provided little protection against the cold and many Cherokee became sick.

By this time, U.S. general Winfield Scott had become in charge of removing the Cherokee. He was sympathetic to the Cherokee and told the remaining leaders that he hoped to avoid violence. But Scott was determined to carry out the removal. The Cherokee had until May 23, 1838, to voluntarily move to Indian Territory. When this date arrived, there were still an estimated 17,000 Cherokee in the east.

Scott used 7,000 regular and militia troops to round up the Cherokee. He urged the troops to be kind to the Cherokee. The roundup, however, was cruel. When soldiers seized the Cherokee, parents and children often became separated. Many of the Cherokee lost most of their possessions. As they were forced out, white people moved in. These intruders burned Cherokee homes, drove off livestock, and dug up graves to search for silver jewelry.

Soldiers moved the Cherokee into more than 20 stockades. Conditions in the stockades were horrible. There was little clean drinking water or healthy food.

Donald Vann's painting Leaving the Memories
illustrates the harsh winter on the Trail of Tears.

The stockades also did not offer much shelter against the rain and sun. Health problems became widespread. Malnutrition, dysentery, whooping cough, fever, and other diseases afflicted the Cherokee. No one knows exactly how many Cherokee captives died during the roundup and in the stockades. Estimates range from 2,000 to 3,000.

In June 1838, hundreds of Cherokee headed west on boats. But many of them died from diseases now thought to have been caused by contaminated water or bacterial infections. Later in June, dry weather made boat travel on the rivers impossible. The Cherokee chiefs requested that removal be delayed until September.

Meanwhile, another change occurred with the Cherokee removal. Ross insisted that the Cherokee should be in charge of the move west.

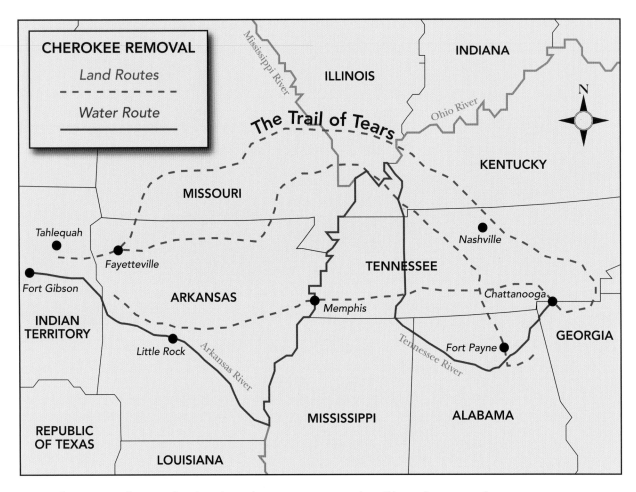

This map shows the land and water routes the Cherokee used to move west.

The U.S. War Department turned over responsibility of the removal to Ross. He negotiated an agreement with General Scott in which each Cherokee received $65 to cover the costs of moving west. In addition, Scott furnished wagons, horses, and oxen for the move.

Not all the remaining Cherokee proceeded west under Ross's supervision. A group who favored the Treaty of New Echota left in October. They traveled through Tennessee and Arkansas and arrived at their new territory in January 1839.

The Cherokee under Ross's management took a more northern route chosen by Scott. This path went across Tennessee into Kentucky and then across southern Illinois and Missouri. These Cherokee left in 13 groups that ranged from about 200 members to well over 1,000. The route generally took about 116 days to complete. This path became known as the Trail of Tears.

A soldier named John G. Burnett later recalled the Cherokee removal. He remembered Chief Junaluska's reaction to the heartbreaking events. The chief regretted saving Jackson's life at the Battle of Horseshoe Bend.

The Native Americans on this trail endured their long trek during winter. They were miserable as they proceeded in the cold. Again, the Cherokee faced a host of serious health problems. They suffered from pneumonia, tuberculosis, cholera, and dysentery.

Hundreds of Cherokee died on the Trail of Tears. Anywhere from 1,000 to 1,500 are believed to have died while moving west. When deaths from the roundup and stockades are considered as well, about 4,000 Cherokees are believed to have died. Based on these estimates, the removal killed about 20 to 25 percent of the eastern Cherokee.

Among those who became seriously ill was Ross's wife, Quatie. She had given her blanket to a child and soon got pneumonia. Ross decided to move his family the rest of the way by boat. They moved up the Mississippi and Arkansas rivers along with another group of Cherokee. Quatie died February 1, 1839, near Little Rock, Arkansas. Ross buried her and then proceeded to Indian Territory with the survivors.

INDIAN TERRITORY

The Cherokee continued to experience troubles when they arrived in Indian Territory. Bitterness over the Treaty of New Echota divided the tribe. The treaty supporters were still led by Major Ridge, John Ridge, and Elias Boudinot. John Ross continued to head the Cherokee opposed to the treaty.

A constitutional convention was scheduled in June 1839. Its purpose was to unite the hostile groups. But before the convention was held, Major Ridge, John Ridge, and Boudinot were murdered. Ross's supporters committed the violence, though Ross denied playing a role in the assassinations. Stand Watie was also targeted, but he escaped harm. He took over the leadership of those opposed to Ross.

The Cherokee were not the only Native Americans locked in a struggle. In Florida, the Seminole continued to fight the U.S. Army. The United States removed more than 3,000 Seminole to Indian Territory, but hundreds of Seminole still lived in the Everglades. Also, the American people had become tired of the war. About 2,000 U.S. soldiers had died in a conflict that had cost the country more than $40,000,000. In 1842, the United States quit fighting the Seminole remaining in the Everglades.

The Cherokee also saw an end to their conflict. In 1846, the United States compelled the Cherokee to reach an agreement to stop

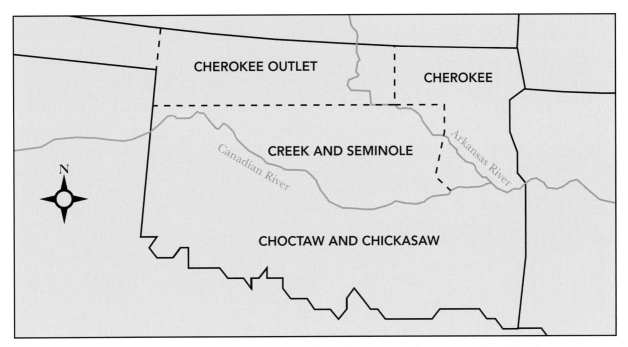

This map shows the land that the Cherokee, Creek, Seminole, Choctaw, and Chickasaw received in Indian Territory, including the Cherokee Outlet.

the violence. The end of this strife allowed the tribe to experience a few years of calm in the 1850s. Once again, the Cherokee became successful farmers. However, they had to endure a different environment in Indian Territory. Temperatures were more extreme. Drought and floods were both common.

The United States government and white settlers benefited from the removal policy that caused so much hardship for the Native Americans. Millions of acres of land came into the possession of the United States. The U.S. government had acquired this land cheaply and sold it to settlers for a higher price.

The removal of Native Americans is considered a shameful event in U.S. history. One unidentified guard at the stockades remembered the awful conditions there. The guard compared the camps with the Civil War fought more than 20 years later. He wrote, "During the Civil War I watched as hundreds of men died, including my own brother, but none of that compares to what we did to the Cherokee Indians."

TIMELINE

1732 King George II issues a charter to establish the Georgia colony.

1754 to 1763 England and France and their Native American allies fight the French and Indian War. England defeats France for control of much of North America.

1763 King George III announces the Proclamation of 1763 which bars English colonists from moving west of the Appalachian Mountains.

1775 to 1783 The 13 American colonies revolt against British rule in the Revolutionary War.

1812 to 1814 The United States and Britain fight the War of 1812.

1814 On March 27, U.S. forces and Native Americans defeat the Red Sticks at the Battle of Horseshoe Bend.

On August 9, Creek leaders cede 23 million acres (9 million ha) to the United States in the Treaty of Fort Jackson.

1821 Sequoyah presents his syllabary to Cherokee chiefs.

1827 The Cherokee adopt a constitution.

1829 In July, gold is discovered on Cherokee land.

In December, President Andrew Jackson advocates removing Native Americans to land west of the Mississippi River.

1830 In May, the Indian Removal Act becomes law.

1832 On March 3, the U.S. Supreme Court issues a decision on *Worcester v. Georgia*. The Court rules that states do not have authority over Native American nations.

1835 In December, the U.S. government and a minority of the Cherokee negotiate the Treaty of New Echota.

1835 to 1842 The United States and the Seminole fight the Second Seminole War in Florida.

1838 to 1839 Thousands of Cherokee are rounded up and forced to travel hundreds of miles on the Trail of Tears.

American Moments

FAST FACTS

The Indian Removal Act eventually led to the relocation of more than 100,000 Native Americans.

Some Cherokee managed to remain in the eastern United States. During the roundup of the tribe, hundreds of Cherokee escaped into the mountains of western North Carolina. The U.S. government eventually decided to allow these Cherokee to remain there. Today, this group is called the Eastern Band of Cherokee.

Many Cherokee brought their slaves to Indian Territory. Cherokee who owned slaves generally had an easier journey. Slaves performed many duties during the move west, including clearing trails, cooking, and driving teams of horses.

The Cherokee and Choctaw wanted to name a state after Sequoyah. In the early twentieth century, there was a move to admit the Oklahoma Territory as a state. Two chiefs proposed a separate state for land held by Native Americans. This state would be named Sequoyah. The plan, however, never became a reality.

In 1987, Congress made the Trail of Tears a National Historic Trail. The National Parks Service supervises the trail.

WEB SITES
WWW.ABDOPUB.COM

Would you like to learn more about the Trail of Tears? Please visit **www.abdopub.com** to find up-to-date Web site links about the Trail of Tears and other American moments. These links are routinely monitored and updated to provide the most current information available.

(Clockwise from top left): *Seals of the Creek (Muskogee), Chickasaw, Choctaw, and Cherokee nations.*

GLOSSARY

American Board of Commissioners for Foreign Missions: a New England
  missionary organization established in 1810. The board sent missionaries
  to foreign countries and to Native American tribes in the United States.

assassinate: to murder a very important person.

cede: to give up possession of something by treaty.

charter: a written contract that states a colony's boundaries and forms of
  government.

cholera: a disease of the intestines that includes severe vomiting and diarrhea.

Civil War: a war between groups in the same country. The United States of
  America and the Confederate States of America fought a civil war from
  1861 to 1865.

confederacy: a group of people joined together for a common purpose.

constitution: the laws that govern a country.

drought: a long period of dry weather.

dysentery: a disease that causes severe diarrhea.

Everglades: a large marsh in southern Florida.

flatboat: a boat similar to a raft. Flatboats were mainly used to transport
  freight.

House of Representatives: the lower house in the U.S. Congress.
  Citizens elect members of the house to make laws for the nation.

immune: having resistance to disease.

Industrial Revolution: the period in the eighteenth and nineteenth centuries when the world economy was changed by the addition of new technology and machinery.

jurisdiction: an area where a particular group has the power to govern or enforce laws.

malaria: a disease spread by mosquitoes that causes chills and fever.

malnutrition: not getting enough essential food elements such as vitamins and minerals to keep one's body healthy.

militia: a group of people trained for war or emergencies.

missionary: a person who spreads a church's religion.

negotiate: to settle an issue through discussion.

pneumonia: a disease of the lungs that includes coughing, fever, chest pain, and chills.

Revolutionary War: 1775 to 1783. A war for independence between England and its North American colonies. The colonists won and created the United States.

Senate: the upper house in the U.S. Congress. The Senate has two members from each state in the Union. They make laws for the country.

smallpox: a disease that causes a blister-like skin rash, vomiting, fever, and fatigue. The blisters become scars.

Supreme Court: the highest, most powerful court in the United States.

syllabary: a writing system in which symbols represent syllables.

tuberculosis: a bacterial infection of oxygen-rich areas of the body such as the lungs.

War of 1812: 1812 to 1814. A war fought between the United States and Great Britain over shipping rights and the capture of U.S. soldiers.

whooping cough: a bacterial infection of the lungs that includes severe coughing.

INDEX